Animals and Their Adaptations

Kate Boehm Jerome

PICTURE CREDITS

Cover (front), Steven Nourse/Accent Alaska; pages 1, 35 (third from top), Digital Vision/ Getty Images Inc.; pages 2-3, 11, 25 (bottom left), 35 (second from top), 33, Photodisc Green/Getty Images Inc.; pages 4-5 (top left), 31 (bottom left), IT Stock Free/PictureQuest; pages 4-5 (bottom left), 31 (bottom right), Photodisc Blue/Getty Images; page 5 (top), Image State/PictureQuest; pages 5 (bottom), 6-7, 28 (top), 32, Stone/Getty Images, Inc.; pages 7 (top), © Buddy Mays/Corbis; pages 8, 31 (top right), Joyce Photographics/ Photo Researchers, Inc.; pages 9 (top and bottom), 25 (top left), 26 (top), 28 (bottom), 30 (top right), The Image Bank/Getty Images, Inc.; pages 10, 31 (center left), 34 (top), Tom Brakefield/Corbis; pages 12, 25 (top right), 26 (bottom), 35 (bottom), Taxi/Getty Images, Inc.; page 13 (top left); Farrell Grehan/Corbis; page 13 (top right), Gavriel Jecan/Corbis; page 13 (bottom left), Stephen Frink/Corbis; page 13 (bottom right), Joe McDonald/Visuals Unlimited; page 15, Joel Sartore/National Geographic Image Collection; pages 14, 25 (bottom right), 27, 29 (bottom), 31 (top left), 35 (top), Royalty-Free/Corbis; pages 16-17; 18, 19 (top), 34 (bottom), E. Widder/HBOI/Visuals Unlimited; page 19 (bottom), David Wrobel/Visuals Unlimited; page 20 (left and right), Kim Reisenbichler MBARI; pages 21, 30 (bottom right), 34 (second from top), Y.Kito/imagequestmarine.com; pages 22, 34 (third from top), Southampton Oceanography Center/imagequestmarine.com; page 23, Dr. Paul A. Zahl /Photo Researchers, Inc.; pages 29 (top), 30 (bottom left), Steve Kaufman/Corbis; page 31 (top right), John Conrad/Corbis; page 36, National Geographic/Getty Images, Inc.

Produced through the worldwide resources of the National Geographic Society, John M. Fahey, Jr., President and Chief Executive Officer; Gilbert M. Grosvenor, Chairman of the Board; Nina D. Hoffman, Executive Vice President and President, Books and Education Publishing Group.

PREPARED BY NATIONAL GEOGRAPHIC SCHOOL PUBLISHING

Ericka Markman, Senior Vice President and President, Children's Books and Education Publishing Group; Steve Mico, Senior Vice President, Editorial Director, Publisher; Francis Downey, Executive Editor; Richard Easby, Editorial Manager; Bea Jackson, Director of Layout and Design; Jim Hiscott, Design Manager; Cynthia Olson, Art Director; Margaret Sidlosky, Illustrations Director; Matt Wascavage, Manager of Publishing Services; Sean Philpotts, Jane Ponton, Production Managers; Ted Tucker, Production Specialist.

MANUFACTURING AND QUALITY CONTROL

Christopher A. Liedel, Chief Financial Officer; Phillip L. Schlosser, Director; Clifton M. Brown III, Manager

CONSULTANTS AND REVIEWERS

Kefyn M. Catley, Ph.D., Assistant Professor of Science Education, Department of Teaching and Learning, Peabody College, Assistant Professor of Biology, Vanderbilt University, Research Associate, Division of Invertebrate Zoology, American Museum of Natural History, New York

Julie Edmonds, Associate Director, Carnegie Academy for Science Education, Carnegie Institution of Washington

◄ A baby orangutan reaches for a branch in a rain forest of Indonesia.

Contents

BOOK DEVELOPMENT
Amy Sarver

BOOK DESIGN/PHOTO RESEARCH
3R1 Group, Inc.

Published by the National Geographic Society
1145 17th Street N.W.
Washington, D.C. 20036-4688

ISBN: 0-7922-5404-X

2016
6 7 8 9 10 11 12 13 14 15

Printed in USA

Awesome Animals

▲ **Elephants can use their trunks to move water into their mouths.**

The world is full of amazing animals. Each kind of animal has special features and behaviors. For example, tigers have stripes that help them hide when they hunt. Sharks have sharp teeth for eating other animals. Different features and behaviors help animals **survive**.

Look at the pictures.

- What features do you see?
- How do those features help each animal survive?
- What are the elephants doing?
- How does this behavior help the elephants survive?

· ·
survive – to stay alive

▲ **A tiger's black stripes help it hide.**

4

▲ A shark uses its sharp teeth to eat other animals.

▲ A fox has thick fur that helps keep it warm.

Big Idea

Adaptations are important to an animal's survival.

Set Purpose

Think about how features and behaviors help animals to survive.

What Helps Animals Surviv

What are adaptations?

Why are adaptations important to an animal's survival?

Animals survive because of special features or behaviors called **adaptations**. A body part of an animal can be an adaptation. The way an animal acts can also be an adaptation.

Adaptations help animals to do many things.

- Adaptations help animals live in their **habitats,** or homes.
- Adaptations help animals get food.
- Adaptations help animals avoid being eaten.
- Adaptations help animals find mates.

In this book, you will learn why adaptations are important to an animal's survival.

....

adaptation – a feature or behavior that helps a living thing survive

habitat – the place where a plant or animal lives

Adaptations and Habitats

Could a camel live underwater? Of course not! Why? Camels are not adapted to live in such a place.

Camels do have adaptations that help them live in the desert. They have wide feet that keep them from sinking in the sand. Camels also have fatty humps. The humps can let camels go for weeks without food. These adaptations are perfect for life in a hot desert.

▼ A camel's hump and feet are adaptations that help it to live in the desert.

hump

foot

Living Where It Is Hot or Cold

Collared lizards also live in deserts. But they do not have feet like camels. These lizards have feet with long toes. Their toes lift the lizard off the hot sand. This helps keep the lizard cool.

Some animals have adaptations that help them live in cold places. Think about a polar bear. It has a heavy coat of fur. That keeps the bear warm. Different adaptations help animals live in different places.

▼ A collared lizard's long toes help it survive in the desert.

toes

◄ A polar bear's fur helps it live where it is very cold.

Getting Food

A long, sticky tongue and big, sharp claws are important adaptations of an anteater. A giant anteater sniffs out ant nests on the forest floor. It uses its sharp claws to rip open the ant nests. Then it flicks its sticky tongue into the nest to catch the ants.

▼ An anteater rips open an ant nest.

claw

ant nest

Catching Dinner

It is easy to spot an adaptation such as sharp claws. But adaptations are not just body parts. They can also be ways an animal acts.

A mountain lion is a strong animal. Yet it cannot just use its strength to catch dinner. It also has behaviors that help it hunt. A mountain lion walks quietly toward an animal. It gets very close. Then it chases the animal. This helps a mountain lion catch its meal.

▼ **A mountain lion looks for a meal.**

Hiding Out

Adaptations can help some animals hide from **predators.** Predators are animals that hunt and eat other animals.

Can you see the animal in the picture below? It is a chameleon. It looks like the leaves on the tree. This adaptation makes the chameleon hard to see. Its color helps it hide from predators.

predator – an animal that hunts and eats other animals

▼ **A chameleon hides in a tree.**

Staying Safe

Many adaptations help animals stay safe. Some have to do with how an animal looks. Others have to do with how an animal acts. The chart shows some ways animals stay safe.

Animal Survival

A grasshopper's color helps it hide.

A zebra runs fast to get away.

A porcupine fish puffs up to scare predators away.

An opossum plays dead to trick predators.

Finding a Mate

Animals need mates. Why? So they can **reproduce,** or have young. If a kind of animal could not have young, that kind of animal would die out. So finding a mate is important.

Some adaptations help animals battle for a mate. Just look at the male white-tailed deer. It grows huge antlers. A male deer uses its antlers to fight other male deer. The winner of the battle often wins a mate.

....

reproduce – to have young or make more of one's own kind

▼ **A male deer has antlers that help it win a mate.**

antlers

Dancing for a Mate

Special behaviors also help an animal find a mate. The male Attwater prairie chicken does a special mating dance. It holds its tail high and drops its wings. It blows up an air sac under its beak. Then it drops its head and forces air out of the sac. This makes a low sound. Finally, the prairie chicken stomps its feet very fast. These behaviors help it find a mate.

Stop and Think!

How are adaptations important to an animal's survival?

▼ A male Attwater prairie chicken dances to find a mate.

air sac

15

Recap
Explain why adaptations are important.

Set Purpose
Learn about adaptations of animals that live deep in the ocean.

Monsters F

You know that adaptations can be helpful in many ways. You also know that some adaptations may seem a bit weird. But you have not seen anything yet. Wait until you meet the creatures in the deep sea!

om the Deep

Into the Deep

In the shallow layers of the ocean, there are many plants and colorful fish. But the deeper you go in the ocean, the more things change. The water gets colder. It also gets darker as less sunlight gets through.

At about 100 meters (330 feet) there is not enough light for plants to grow. Below this, light fades even more. At about 914 meters (3,000 feet) down, there is no sunlight at all.

▼ This animal lives in the deep ocean where there is no sunlight.

Life in the Dark

Some animals live in total darkness. How do they find food in the dark? Adaptations help them.

Many deep-sea creatures have special **cells** in their bodies. These cells make light. A flash of light in the dark often **attracts** other fish. This makes it easier for an animal to catch its dinner!

Razor-sharp teeth are also a common adaptation. Down in the dark water, every bite is important.

cell – the basic unit of living things

attract – to make other things come near

▲ A dragonfish has cells that make light.

▼ A fangtooth has sharp teeth.

Spikes That Protect

The vampire squid's name sounds spooky. But its name does not protect it from predators. Adaptations do. It has tooth-shaped spikes that cover the inside of its arms. It uses these spikes to protect itself from predators.

When a predator comes by, this squid turns itself inside out. Then the squid's spikes are on the outside of its body. The spikes help the squid stay safe.

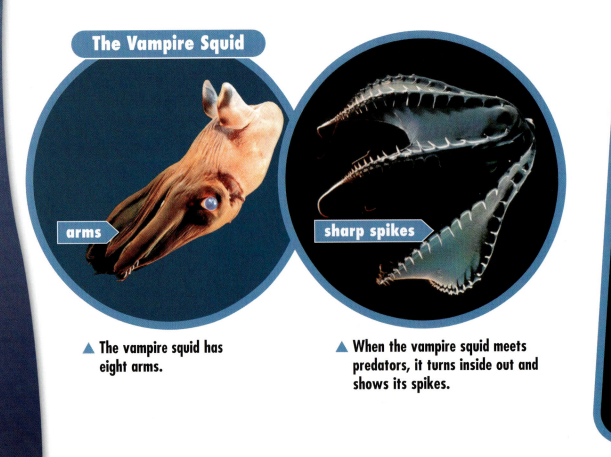

The Vampire Squid

arms

sharp spikes

▲ The vampire squid has eight arms.

▲ When the vampire squid meets predators, it turns inside out and shows its spikes.

Glowing in the Dark

The firefly squid is another deep-sea animal. This squid is only eight centimeters (three inches) long. But it has cells that can make a lot of light.

The firefly squid can flash its light to attract food. It can also make its whole body glow. This comes in handy when the squid is trying to attract a mate.

▼ A firefly squid has cells that glow in the dark ocean.

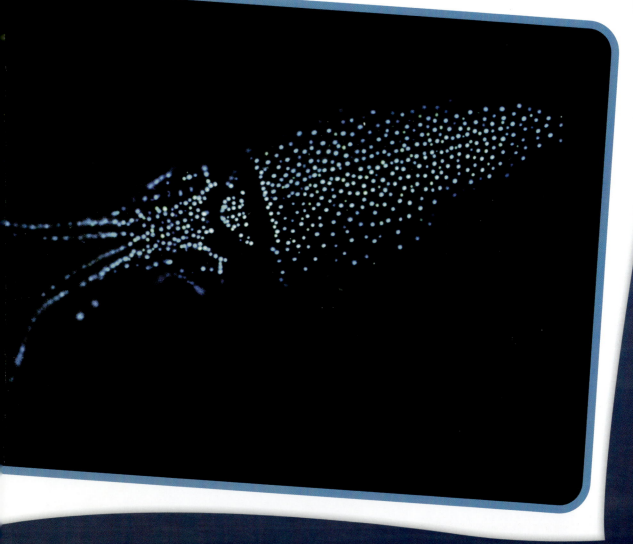

Deep-sea Fishing

Imagine a fish that fishes! Anglerfish look like they have a built-in fishing pole. It is really part of a fin. It attracts food.

The tip of the "fishing pole" holds millions of special **bacteria.** They make light. The anglerfish waves the light. Small animals swim to it. Then they end up as dinner.

▼ An anglerfish has a fishing pole with a light.

bacteria – tiny living things made of only one cell

A Light in the Dark

Many adaptations help animals survive in the deep sea. For example, a viperfish has a dark-colored body. This makes its body hard to see. Yet viperfish can make light. Fish swim toward the light. But they do not know they are swimming toward the hungry viperfish's dangerous mouth. The viperfish's adaptations help it live in the deep ocean.

▼ A viperfish has cells that make light and a body that is dark in color.

Stop and Think!

How do adaptations help deep-sea creatures survive?

Recap
Explain why adaptations are important.

Set Purpose
Read these articles to learn more about adaptations.

CONNECT WHAT YOU HAVE LEARNED

Animal Adaptations

Do you know what all animals have in common? They have adaptations. Adaptations help animals survive in their habitats.

Here are some ideas you learned about animal adaptations.

- Each kind of animal has body features and behaviors that help it survive.
- These features and behaviors are called adaptations.
- Adaptations help animals live in their habitats, protect themselves, find food, and find mates.

Check What You Have Learned

How do adaptations help the animals in the photos survive?

▲ Adaptations help animals live in their habitats.

▲ Adaptations help animals hide.

▲ Adaptations help animals find food.

▲ Adaptations help animals find mates.

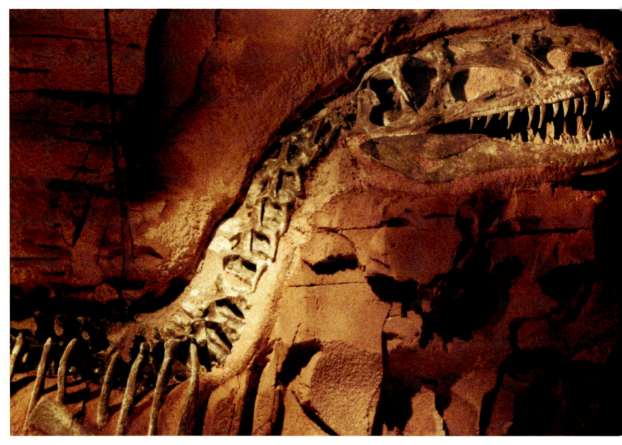

▲ **A dinosaur fossil is in this rock.**

Fossil Clues

Fossils are signs of past life. They tell about plants and animals that lived long ago. They help scientists learn about the past. Sometimes fossils show adaptations of plants or animals that lived long ago.

▶ **This is a fossil of a dinosaur with wings.**

26

Losing Wild Habitats

Some animals have a shaky future in the wild. This is true for the koala. The koala adapted to eat the leaves of certain eucalyptus trees. In fact, these leaves are about the only food a koala will eat.

So what is the problem? The eucalyptus trees are disappearing. People are cutting down the trees. They are clearing land for farms and houses. This means the koala is losing its habitat. It is losing its food source in the wild.

► A koala eats the leaves of this eucalyptus tree.

Zoos Care for Animals

Making zoo animals feel at "home" is not easy. Most modern zoos try to build displays that are like the animals' natural homes. In some zoos, polar bears have cool pools for swimming. Orangutans have ropes to climb. Natural displays allow animals to use many of their adaptations as they would in the wild.

▶ Zoos have cool pools for polar bears.

▲ Zoos have ropes for orangutans to climb.

▲ **Garter snakes stay close together to keep warm.**

Sleeping Snakes

Garter snakes are one of the most common kinds of snake. These snakes often lie in the sun to keep their bodies warm. But when winter sets in, they need to take cover.

Some garter snakes travel for miles to find a den in winter. Hundreds of snakes can gather together in one den. Keeping their bodies close helps keep them warm. So when spring arrives, they are ready to hunt and mate.

Many kinds of words are used in this book. Here you will learn about nouns. You will also learn about adjectives.

Nouns

A noun is a word that names a person, animal, place, or thing. Find the nouns below. Then use each noun in your own sentence.

An **orangutan** holds a plant.

This **lizard** lives in the desert.

These **snakes** gather together in a den.

This **squid** has cells that make light.

Adjectives

An adjective is a word that describes a noun or a pronoun. An adjective often goes before the word it describes. Find the adjectives below. Use each adjective in your own sentence.

Polar bears have a **heavy** coat of fur.

A camel has **wide** feet.

An anteater has a **sticky** tongue.

A mountain lion has **sharp** claws.

Elephants have **long** trunks.

This deer has **huge** antlers.

Write About Animal Adaptations

Choose an animal to research. Find out about the animal's adaptations. Then write an informational report telling what you learned.

Research

Collect books and reference materials, or go online.

Read and Take Notes

As you read, take notes and draw pictures.

Write

Then write about the animal's adaptations. Draw pictures showing the adaptations and label each one.

Read More About Animal Adaptations

Find and read other books about animals. As you read, think about these questions.

- How do an animal's body parts help it survive?
- How does an animal's behavior help it survive?
- How do scientists study animals?

Books to Read

NATIONAL GEOGRAPHIC
READING EXPEDITIONS
LIFE SCIENCE
Animal Adaptations
PETER WINKLER

NATIONAL GEOGRAPHIC
READING EXPEDITIONS
LIFE SCIENCE
Classification Clues
CATHERINE STEPHENS

NATIONAL GEOGRAPHIC
READING EXPEDITIONS
LIFE SCIENCE
Amazing Animals
KATE BOEHM NYQUIST

▲ Read how adaptations help animals survive.

▲ Read about ways to classify animals.

▲ Read about animal features and behaviors.

Glossary

adaptation (page 7)
A feature or behavior that helps a living thing survive
An anteater's sticky tongue is an adaptation that helps it find food.

attract (page 19)
To make other things come near
The firefly squid can flash its light to attract food.

bacteria (page 22)
Tiny living things made of only one cell
The bacteria at the tip of the anglerfish's "fishing pole" make light.

cell (page 19)
The basic unit of living things
A dragonfish has special cells that make light.

habitat (page 7)
The place where a plant or animal lives
The eucalyptus tree is an important part of the koala's habitat.

predator (page 12)
An animal that hunts and eats other animals
The mountain lion is a predator.

reproduce (page 14)
To have young or make more of one's own kind
Adaptations help animals reproduce.

survive (page 4)
To stay alive
Hiding in the leaves helps the chameleon survive.

Index